50 German Recipes for Home

By: Kelly Johnson

Table of Contents

- Wiener Schnitzel (Breaded and Fried Veal Cutlet)
- Sauerbraten (Marinated Pot Roast)
- Bratwurst with Sauerkraut
- Pretzels with Beer Cheese Dip
- Kartoffelsalat (German Potato Salad)
- Rouladen (Beef Rolls with Mustard and Pickles)
- Schweinshaxe (Roasted Pork Knuckle)
- Apfelstrudel (Apple Strudel)
- Sauerkraut and Sausage Casserole
- Königsberger Klopse (Meatballs in Caper Sauce)
- Currywurst (Grilled Sausage with Curry Ketchup)
- Rotkohl (Red Cabbage)
- Kartoffelsuppe (Potato Soup)
- Rösti (Swiss Potato Pancakes)
- Hackbraten (German Meatloaf)
- Hühnerfrikassee (Creamy Chicken Fricassee)
- Grünkohl mit Pinkel (Kale with Smoked Sausage)
- Erbsensuppe (Pea Soup)
- Lebkuchen (German Gingerbread Cookies)
- Spätzle (Egg Noodles)
- Labskaus (Corned Beef Hash)
- Leberknödel Suppe (Liver Dumpling Soup)
- Schwarzwälder Kirschtorte (Black Forest Cake)
- Gulaschsuppe (Goulash Soup)
- Himmel und Erde (Heaven and Earth - Potatoes and Apples)
- Quarkkuchen (German Cheesecake)
- Dampfnudeln (Steamed Sweet Dumplings)
- Heringsalat (Herring Salad)
- Reibekuchen (Potato Pancakes)
- Kartoffelkloesse (Potato Dumplings)
- Zwiebelkuchen (Onion Tart)
- Fischbrötchen (Fish Sandwich)
- Zimtsterne (Cinnamon Stars Cookies)
- Schupfnudeln (Potato Noodles)
- Weißwurst mit Brezn (White Sausage with Pretzel)

- Gemüsesuppe (Vegetable Soup)
- Maultaschen (Swabian Dumplings)
- Birnen, Bohnen und Speck (Pears, Beans, and Bacon)
- Krustenbraten (Roast Pork with Crispy Skin)
- Rhabarberkuchen (Rhubarb Cake)
- Bienenstich (Bee Sting Cake)
- Schmandkuchen (Sour Cream Cake)
- Blumenkohl in Senfsauce (Cauliflower in Mustard Sauce)
- Weihnachtsplätzchen (Christmas Cookies)
- Rinderrouladen (Beef Rolls with Bacon and Pickles)
- Senfeier (Mustard Eggs)
- Wurstsalat (Sausage Salad)
- Linsensuppe (Lentil Soup)
- Stollen (German Christmas Fruitcake)
- Kaiserschmarrn (Shredded Pancakes)

Wiener Schnitzel (Breaded and Fried Veal Cutlet)

Ingredients:

- 4 veal cutlets (about 1/4 inch thick)
- Salt and black pepper, to taste
- All-purpose flour, for dredging
- 2 large eggs
- 1 cup breadcrumbs (preferably fresh)
- Vegetable oil, for frying
- Lemon wedges, for serving

Instructions:

1. Prepare the Veal Cutlets:

    If the veal cutlets are thick, you can use a meat mallet to pound them to an even thickness of about 1/4 inch.
    Season the veal cutlets with salt and black pepper on both sides.

2. Set Up Dredging Stations:

    Place the flour on a plate for dredging.
    In a shallow bowl, beat the eggs.
    Place the breadcrumbs on another plate.

3. Dredge and Bread the Cutlets:

    Dredge each veal cutlet in flour, shaking off any excess.
    Dip the cutlet into the beaten eggs, ensuring it is coated evenly.
    Press the cutlet into the breadcrumbs, making sure it is well-coated on both sides.

4. Fry the Cutlets:

    In a large skillet, heat enough vegetable oil to cover the bottom of the pan over medium-high heat.
    Once the oil is hot, carefully place the breaded veal cutlets into the pan.

Fry each cutlet for about 3-4 minutes on each side or until golden brown and cooked through.
Place the fried cutlets on a paper towel-lined plate to absorb any excess oil.

5. Serve:

- Serve the Wiener Schnitzel hot, garnished with lemon wedges on the side for squeezing over the cutlets.

6. Optional: Garnish and Sides:

- Garnish the Wiener Schnitzel with parsley if desired.
- Serve with your choice of sides, such as potato salad, lingonberry sauce, or a simple green salad.

Wiener Schnitzel is best enjoyed immediately while the breading is crispy. The lemon wedges add a refreshing citrusy touch to complement the richness of the veal. This dish is a favorite in German and Austrian cuisine and is sure to be a hit at your table!

Sauerbraten (Marinated Pot Roast)

Ingredients:

For the Marinade:

- 3 lbs (about 1.4 kg) beef roast (chuck or rump)
- 1 large onion, sliced
- 1 carrot, sliced
- 1 leek, sliced
- 2 bay leaves
- 10 whole cloves
- 10 whole black peppercorns
- 1 teaspoon mustard seeds
- 1 cup red wine vinegar
- 1 cup red wine
- 2 cups water
- 2 tablespoons salt
- 2 tablespoons sugar

For Cooking:

- 2 tablespoons vegetable oil
- 2 onions, sliced
- 2 tablespoons all-purpose flour
- 2 cups beef broth
- 2 tablespoons red currant jelly (optional)
- Salt and pepper, to taste

Instructions:

1. Marinate the Meat:

   Place the beef roast in a large bowl or resealable plastic bag.
   In a saucepan, combine the sliced onion, carrot, leek, bay leaves, cloves, peppercorns, mustard seeds, red wine vinegar, red wine, water, salt, and sugar.
   Bring the marinade to a boil, then let it cool to room temperature.
   Pour the cooled marinade over the beef roast, ensuring it's fully submerged.
   Marinate in the refrigerator for at least 2 days, turning the meat occasionally.

2. Cook the Sauerbraten:

Preheat the oven to 325°F (163°C).
Remove the beef from the marinade and pat it dry with paper towels. Reserve the marinade.
In a Dutch oven or large oven-safe pot, heat vegetable oil over medium-high heat. Brown the beef on all sides, then remove it from the pot.

3. Sauté Onions and Make Roux:

    Add sliced onions to the pot and sauté until they are softened.
    Sprinkle flour over the onions and stir to create a roux.

4. Add Marinade and Broth:

    Pour the reserved marinade over the onions and roux.
    Add beef broth and red currant jelly (if using).
    Stir well to combine.

5. Cook in the Oven:

    - Return the browned beef to the pot.
    - Cover the pot and transfer it to the preheated oven.
    - Braise the Sauerbraten for about 2.5 to 3 hours or until the meat is tender.

6. Serve:

    - Remove the beef from the pot, slice it, and serve with the sauce.
    - Strain the sauce if desired, and adjust the seasoning with salt and pepper.

7. Optional: Gravy:

    - If you desire a thicker sauce, you can create a gravy by thickening the sauce with a cornstarch slurry.

Sauerbraten is often served with traditional side dishes like potato dumplings (Kartoffelklöße) or boiled potatoes and red cabbage. Enjoy this flavorful and comforting German pot roast!

Bratwurst with Sauerkraut

Ingredients:

- 4 Bratwurst sausages
- 1 pound (about 500g) sauerkraut, drained
- 1 large onion, thinly sliced
- 2 tablespoons vegetable oil
- 1 teaspoon caraway seeds
- 1 cup (240ml) chicken or vegetable broth
- Salt and black pepper, to taste
- Mustard, for serving (optional)
- Fresh parsley, chopped, for garnish (optional)

Instructions:

1. Preheat Grill or Skillet:

- Preheat your grill or a large skillet over medium-high heat.

2. Grill Bratwurst:

Grill the Bratwurst sausages until they are cooked through and have a golden-brown exterior. This usually takes about 10-15 minutes, turning occasionally.

3. Sauté Onions and Prepare Sauerkraut:

While the sausages are grilling, heat vegetable oil in a large skillet over medium heat.
Add sliced onions and sauté until they become soft and golden.
Add the sauerkraut to the skillet and cook for a few minutes until it's heated through.

4. Season and Add Caraway Seeds:

- Season the sauerkraut mixture with caraway seeds, salt, and black pepper according to your taste.

5. Add Broth:

    Pour the chicken or vegetable broth over the sauerkraut mixture.
    Allow the mixture to simmer for about 10-15 minutes, allowing the flavors to meld.

6. Serve:

    Place the grilled Bratwurst on a serving plate.
    Spoon the sauerkraut mixture over the Bratwurst.
    Garnish with fresh parsley if desired.
    Serve hot with mustard on the side if you like.

7. Optional: Buns or Bread:

- Bratwurst with Sauerkraut can also be served in buns or with slices of crusty bread.

Enjoy this hearty and flavorful Bratwurst with Sauerkraut dish, a delicious representation of traditional German cuisine!

Pretzels with Beer Cheese Dip

Soft Pretzels:

Ingredients:

- 1 ½ cups warm water (110°F/43°C)
- 1 tablespoon sugar
- 2 teaspoons salt
- 1 package (2 ¼ teaspoons) active dry yeast
- 4 ½ cups all-purpose flour
- 4 tablespoons unsalted butter, melted
- Cooking spray, for greasing
- 10 cups water
- 2/3 cup baking soda
- 1 large egg yolk beaten with 1 tablespoon water, for brushing
- Coarse salt, for sprinkling

Instructions:

1. Make the Pretzel Dough:

    In a bowl, combine warm water, sugar, and salt. Sprinkle the yeast over the water mixture and let it sit for 5 minutes, or until it becomes foamy.
    In a large mixing bowl, combine the flour and melted butter. Pour in the yeast mixture and mix until a dough forms.
    Knead the dough on a floured surface for about 5 minutes until it becomes smooth and elastic.
    Place the dough in a greased bowl, cover it with a clean kitchen towel, and let it rise in a warm place for about 1 hour or until it doubles in size.

2. Shape and Boil the Pretzels:

    Preheat your oven to 450°F (232°C).
    Bring 10 cups of water and baking soda to a rolling boil in a large pot.
    Divide the dough into 8 equal pieces. Roll each piece into a long rope and shape it into a pretzel.
    Boil each pretzel in the water-baking soda mixture for 30 seconds, then place them on a greased baking sheet.

3. Brush and Bake:

    Brush each pretzel with the beaten egg yolk-water mixture.
    Sprinkle coarse salt over the pretzels.

Bake in the preheated oven for 12-15 minutes or until the pretzels are golden brown.

Beer Cheese Dip

Ingredients:

- 2 tablespoons unsalted butter
- 2 tablespoons all-purpose flour
- 1 cup beer (choose a lager or ale)
- 2 cups sharp cheddar cheese, shredded
- ½ cup cream cheese
- 1 teaspoon Dijon mustard
- ½ teaspoon garlic powder
- Salt and black pepper, to taste

Instructions:

1. Make the Beer Cheese Dip:

> In a saucepan, melt butter over medium heat.
> Stir in flour to make a roux and cook for 1-2 minutes.
> Gradually whisk in the beer until the mixture is smooth.
> Add the shredded cheddar cheese, cream cheese, Dijon mustard, and garlic powder, stirring continuously until the cheese is melted and the mixture is smooth.
> Season with salt and black pepper according to your taste.

2. Serve:

- Serve the warm pretzels with the beer cheese dip.

Enjoy your homemade Pretzels with Beer Cheese Dip – a perfect combination of soft, salty pretzels and a rich, flavorful cheese dip with a hint of beer!

Kartoffelsalat (German Potato Salad)

Ingredients:

- 2 1/2 pounds (about 1.1 kg) waxy potatoes (such as Yukon Gold or red potatoes)
- 6 slices bacon, diced
- 1 large onion, finely chopped
- 1/3 cup (80 ml) apple cider vinegar
- 1 tablespoon Dijon mustard

- 1 teaspoon granulated sugar
- 1/2 cup (120 ml) chicken or vegetable broth
- Salt and black pepper, to taste
- Chopped fresh parsley, for garnish

Instructions:

1. Boil the Potatoes:

    Scrub the potatoes but leave the skin on. Boil them in a large pot of salted water until tender but not mushy. This usually takes about 15-20 minutes, depending on the size of the potatoes.

2. Cook Bacon and Onions:

    While the potatoes are boiling, cook the diced bacon in a large skillet over medium heat until crispy.
    Add finely chopped onions to the skillet and cook until they are soft and golden.

3. Make the Dressing:

    In a small bowl, whisk together the apple cider vinegar, Dijon mustard, sugar, and chicken or vegetable broth.

4. Slice and Assemble:

    Drain the boiled potatoes and let them cool slightly. Once cool enough to handle, slice them into 1/4-inch thick rounds.
    Add the sliced potatoes to the skillet with the bacon and onions.

5. Combine and Season:

    Pour the dressing over the potatoes, bacon, and onions.
    Gently toss everything together until well combined.
    Season with salt and black pepper according to your taste.

6. Serve:

- Serve the German Potato Salad warm, garnished with chopped fresh parsley.

German Potato Salad is a delicious side dish that is often served alongside grilled meats or at picnics. The warm, tangy dressing makes it a unique and flavorful alternative to traditional cold potato salads. Enjoy!

Schweinshaxe (Roasted Pork Knuckle)

Ingredients:

- 4 pork knuckles

- Salt, to taste
- Black pepper, to taste
- 2 tablespoons caraway seeds
- 2 tablespoons vegetable oil
- 1 large onion, chopped
- 2 carrots, chopped
- 2 celery stalks, chopped
- 4 cloves garlic, minced
- 2 bay leaves
- 2 sprigs fresh thyme
- 2 cups (480 ml) chicken or vegetable broth
- 1 cup (240 ml) beer (traditional choices include lager or bock)

Instructions:

1. Preheat the Oven:

    - Preheat your oven to 375°F (190°C).

2. Prepare the Pork Knuckles:

    Rinse the pork knuckles and pat them dry with paper towels.
    Score the skin of each knuckle with a sharp knife.
    Season the knuckles generously with salt and black pepper.
    Rub caraway seeds over the scored skin.

3. Sear the Pork Knuckles:

    Heat vegetable oil in a large oven-safe skillet or Dutch oven over medium-high heat.
    Sear the pork knuckles on all sides until the skin is golden and crispy.

4. Add Vegetables and Aromatics:

    Add chopped onions, carrots, celery, minced garlic, bay leaves, and fresh thyme to the skillet.
    Cook the vegetables until they are slightly softened.

5. Deglaze with Beer:

- Pour the beer into the skillet, deglazing the pan by scraping up any browned bits from the bottom.

6. Add Broth:

    - Pour the chicken or vegetable broth into the skillet, ensuring the pork knuckles are partially submerged.

7. Roast in the Oven:

    Cover the skillet or Dutch oven with a lid or aluminum foil.
    Transfer the skillet to the preheated oven and roast for about 2 to 2.5 hours, or until the pork is tender.

8. Crisp the Skin:

    - For the last 15-20 minutes of cooking, uncover the skillet to allow the skin to crisp up.

9. Serve:

    - Remove the pork knuckles from the oven and let them rest for a few minutes.
    - Serve the Schweinshaxe with the roasted vegetables and pan juices.

Schweinshaxe is often served with traditional sides like sauerkraut, potato dumplings (Kartoffelklöße), or mashed potatoes. Enjoy this hearty and flavorful German dish!

Apfelstrudel (Apple Strudel)

Ingredients:

For the Dough:

- 2 cups (250g) all-purpose flour, plus extra for dusting
- 1/4 cup (60ml) vegetable oil
- 3/4 cup (180ml) warm water
- 1/2 teaspoon salt

For the Filling:

- 4 large apples (such as Granny Smith), peeled, cored, and thinly sliced
- 1/2 cup (100g) granulated sugar
- 1 cup (150g) raisins
- 1 cup (100g) breadcrumbs
- 1/2 cup (120g) unsalted butter, melted
- 2 teaspoons ground cinnamon
- 1/2 cup (60g) chopped walnuts or almonds (optional)
- Powdered sugar, for dusting

Instructions:

1. Prepare the Dough:

   In a bowl, combine the flour and salt. Make a well in the center and pour in the vegetable oil and warm water.
   Mix the ingredients until a soft dough forms.
   Knead the dough on a floured surface until it becomes smooth and elastic. Form it into a ball, coat it with oil, and let it rest in a covered bowl for about 1 hour.

2. Preheat the Oven:

   - Preheat your oven to 350°F (180°C).

3. Roll out the Dough:

   On a floured surface, roll out the dough into a thin, large rectangle.

4. Prepare the Filling:

In a bowl, mix the sliced apples with sugar, raisins, breadcrumbs, melted butter, ground cinnamon, and chopped nuts if using.

Spread the apple filling evenly over the rolled-out dough, leaving a border around the edges.

5. Roll and Seal:

   Carefully roll the dough with the filling into a log or cylinder.
   Seal the edges by pinching them together.

6. Bake:

   Place the rolled strudel on a parchment-lined baking sheet.
   Brush the top with a bit of melted butter.
   Bake in the preheated oven for about 45-50 minutes or until the strudel is golden brown.

7. Serve:

   Allow the Apple Strudel to cool for a few minutes.
   Dust with powdered sugar before serving.
   Slice and serve warm.

8. Optional: Serve with Vanilla Sauce or Whipped Cream:

- Apple Strudel is often enjoyed with a dollop of whipped cream or served with warm vanilla sauce.

Enjoy this delightful Apfelstrudel with its layers of crisp, golden pastry and sweet, spiced apple filling. It's a perfect treat for any occasion!

Sauerkraut and Sausage Casserole

Ingredients:

- 1 pound (450g) smoked sausage or kielbasa, sliced
- 1 large onion, finely chopped
- 2 cloves garlic, minced
- 1 tablespoon vegetable oil
- 1 can (32 ounces/900g) sauerkraut, drained and rinsed
- 1 tablespoon Dijon mustard
- 1 tablespoon brown sugar
- 1 teaspoon caraway seeds (optional)
- Salt and black pepper, to taste
- 1 cup (240ml) chicken broth
- 1 cup (240ml) sour cream
- 1 cup (100g) shredded Swiss cheese
- Chopped fresh parsley, for garnish

Instructions:

1. Preheat the Oven:

- Preheat your oven to 375°F (190°C).

2. Brown the Sausage:

In a large oven-safe skillet, heat vegetable oil over medium-high heat.
Add the sliced sausage and cook until browned on both sides.
Remove the browned sausage from the skillet and set it aside.

3. Sauté Onion and Garlic:

In the same skillet, add chopped onion and garlic. Sauté until the onion becomes translucent.

4. Combine Sauerkraut Mixture:

Add the drained and rinsed sauerkraut to the skillet with onions and garlic.
Stir in Dijon mustard, brown sugar, caraway seeds (if using), salt, and black pepper.
Pour in chicken broth and mix everything well.

5. Add Sausage:

- Return the browned sausage to the skillet, nestling it into the sauerkraut mixture.

6. Bake:

    Place the skillet in the preheated oven and bake for about 25-30 minutes or until the casserole is heated through.

7. Add Sour Cream and Cheese:

    Remove the skillet from the oven.
    Stir in sour cream and sprinkle shredded Swiss cheese over the top.

8. Broil:

    - Place the skillet under the broiler for a few minutes until the cheese is melted and bubbly.

9. Garnish and Serve:

    - Garnish the casserole with chopped fresh parsley before serving.

10. Optional: Serve with Bread or Potatoes:

    - This casserole pairs well with crusty bread or boiled potatoes.

Enjoy this Sauerkraut and Sausage Casserole for a comforting and satisfying meal that brings together the robust flavors of sauerkraut and smoked sausage.

Königsberger Klopse (Meatballs in Caper Sauce)

Ingredients:

For the Meatballs:

- 1 pound (450g) ground veal or a mixture of beef and pork
- 1/2 cup (50g) breadcrumbs
- 1/2 cup (120ml) milk
- 1 small onion, finely chopped
- 1 clove garlic, minced
- 1 egg
- Salt and pepper, to taste
- 1/2 teaspoon ground nutmeg
- 2 tablespoons chopped fresh parsley
- Flour, for coating

For the Caper Sauce:

- 2 tablespoons butter
- 2 tablespoons all-purpose flour
- 2 cups (480ml) beef or vegetable broth
- 1/2 cup (120ml) heavy cream
- 2 tablespoons capers, drained
- 1 tablespoon lemon juice
- Salt and pepper, to taste

Instructions:

1. Prepare the Meatballs:

   In a bowl, combine breadcrumbs and milk. Let it sit for a few minutes until the breadcrumbs absorb the milk.
   In a large mixing bowl, combine ground veal (or beef and pork mixture), soaked breadcrumbs, chopped onion, minced garlic, egg, salt, pepper, nutmeg, and chopped parsley.
   Mix the ingredients until well combined.
   Shape the mixture into small meatballs and coat them lightly with flour.

2. Brown the Meatballs:

   In a large skillet, heat oil over medium-high heat.
   Brown the meatballs on all sides until golden. You may need to do this in batches to avoid overcrowding the skillet.

Once browned, transfer the meatballs to a plate and set them aside.

3. Prepare the Caper Sauce:

    In the same skillet, melt butter over medium heat.
    Stir in flour to create a roux. Cook for a minute or two until it turns golden.
    Gradually whisk in beef or vegetable broth to create a smooth sauce.
    Stir in heavy cream, capers, and lemon juice.
    Season the sauce with salt and pepper to taste.

4. Simmer the Meatballs:

    Return the browned meatballs to the skillet, coating them with the caper sauce.
    Allow the meatballs to simmer in the sauce for about 15-20 minutes, or until they are cooked through.

5. Serve:

    Once the meatballs are cooked, serve them with the caper sauce over a bed of cooked potatoes, rice, or noodles.
    Garnish with additional chopped parsley if desired.

Königsberger Klopse is a comforting and savory dish that brings together the richness of the meatballs with the tanginess of the caper sauce. Enjoy this classic German dish for a delicious and satisfying meal!

Currywurst (Grilled Sausage with Curry Ketchup)

Ingredients:

For the Curry Ketchup:

- 1 cup (240ml) ketchup
- 1 tablespoon curry powder
- 1 tablespoon apple cider vinegar
- 1 tablespoon honey or brown sugar
- Salt and pepper, to taste

For the Sausages:

- 4 bratwurst or German sausages
- 1 tablespoon vegetable oil (for grilling or frying)

Instructions:

1. Prepare the Curry Ketchup:

    In a small saucepan, combine ketchup, curry powder, apple cider vinegar, honey or brown sugar, salt, and pepper.
    Whisk the ingredients together and place the saucepan over medium heat.

2. Simmer the Sauce:

    Bring the mixture to a simmer, stirring frequently.
    Let it simmer for about 5-10 minutes until the sauce thickens and the flavors meld.
    Adjust the seasoning to taste and set the curry ketchup aside.

3. Grill or Fry the Sausages:

    Preheat your grill or a skillet over medium-high heat.
    If grilling, brush the sausages with a bit of vegetable oil. If frying, add oil to the skillet.

Grill or fry the sausages until they are cooked through and have a nice brown exterior. This usually takes about 10-15 minutes, turning them occasionally.

4. Slice the Sausages:

Once the sausages are cooked, you can either leave them whole or slice them into bite-sized pieces.

5. Serve:

Place the grilled or sliced sausages on a plate.
Pour the warm curry ketchup sauce over the sausages.

6. Optional: Garnish:

Optionally, you can sprinkle additional curry powder on top for extra flavor.
Some variations include adding chopped onions or serving with a side of fries.

7. Enjoy:

Currywurst is often served with a side of bread or fries. Enjoy this iconic German street food with its unique blend of curry-flavored ketchup and grilled sausages. It's a delicious and satisfying treat!

Rotkohl (Red Cabbage)

Ingredients:

- 1 medium-sized red cabbage
- 2 apples, peeled, cored, and grated
- 1 onion, finely chopped
- 2 tablespoons vegetable oil or butter
- 1 cup (240ml) red wine
- 1/4 cup (60ml) red wine vinegar
- 2 tablespoons sugar
- 1 teaspoon salt
- 1/2 teaspoon black pepper
- 4 cloves
- 1 bay leaf
- 1 cinnamon stick

Instructions:

1. Prepare the Red Cabbage:

    Remove the outer leaves of the red cabbage, cut it into quarters, and remove the core.
    Finely shred the red cabbage using a sharp knife or a mandoline.

2. Cook the Onion:

    In a large pot or Dutch oven, heat vegetable oil or butter over medium heat.
    Add the finely chopped onion and cook until it becomes translucent.

3. Add Red Cabbage:

    Add the shredded red cabbage to the pot and stir well with the cooked onion.
    Cook for a few minutes until the cabbage starts to wilt.

4. Pour in Red Wine:

    Pour in the red wine and red wine vinegar.
    Stir in sugar, salt, black pepper, cloves, bay leaf, and add the cinnamon stick.

5. Simmer:

Bring the mixture to a simmer.
Reduce the heat to low, cover the pot, and let it simmer for about 45 minutes to 1 hour, stirring occasionally.

6. Add Apples:

   Add the grated apples to the pot and mix them into the cabbage.
   Continue to simmer for an additional 15-20 minutes until the cabbage is tender and flavorful.

7. Adjust Seasoning:

   Taste and adjust the seasoning, adding more sugar, salt, or pepper if needed.

8. Serve:

   Remove the cloves, bay leaf, and cinnamon stick.
   Serve the Rotkohl as a delicious side dish alongside traditional German meals like Sauerbraten or Schnitzel.

Rotkohl is a versatile and flavorful dish that adds a burst of color and taste to your table.

Enjoy this classic German red cabbage recipe!

Kartoffelsuppe (Potato Soup)

Ingredients:

- 1 tablespoon vegetable oil or butter
- 1 onion, finely chopped
- 2 leeks, cleaned and sliced
- 3 carrots, peeled and diced
- 3 celery stalks, diced
- 4 large potatoes, peeled and diced
- 6 cups (1.5 liters) vegetable or chicken broth
- 1 bay leaf
- 1 teaspoon dried thyme
- Salt and pepper, to taste
- 1 cup (240ml) milk or cream (optional)
- Chopped fresh parsley, for garnish

Instructions:

1. Saute Vegetables:

    In a large pot, heat vegetable oil or butter over medium heat.
    Add the chopped onion, leeks, carrots, and celery. Saute until the vegetables are softened, about 5-7 minutes.

2. Add Potatoes and Broth:

    Add the diced potatoes to the pot and pour in the vegetable or chicken broth.
    Add the bay leaf, dried thyme, salt, and pepper to taste.

3. Simmer:

    Bring the soup to a boil, then reduce the heat to low, cover, and simmer for about 15-20 minutes or until the potatoes are tender.

4. Blend (Optional):

    If you prefer a smoother soup, you can use an immersion blender to blend part of the soup until you reach your desired consistency.

5. Add Milk or Cream (Optional):

If desired, stir in milk or cream to add creaminess to the soup. Adjust the seasoning if necessary.

6. Garnish and Serve:

Remove the bay leaf from the soup.
Ladle the Kartoffelsuppe into bowls and garnish with chopped fresh parsley.

7. Serve Warm:

Serve the German Potato Soup warm, optionally with a slice of crusty bread or a sprinkle of additional herbs for added flavor.

Kartoffelsuppe is a delicious and filling soup that showcases the comforting flavors of potatoes and vegetables. Enjoy this traditional German dish as a satisfying meal, especially during chilly weather!

Rösti (Swiss Potato Pancakes)

Ingredients:

- 4 large potatoes, peeled and grated

- 2 tablespoons butter or vegetable oil
- Salt and pepper, to taste

Instructions:

1. Grate the Potatoes:

    Peel the potatoes and grate them using a box grater or a food processor.

2. Squeeze Excess Moisture:

    Place the grated potatoes in a clean kitchen towel or cheesecloth.
    Squeeze out as much moisture as possible from the potatoes.

3. Season:

    Transfer the squeezed potatoes to a bowl.
    Season with salt and pepper to taste. Mix well.

4. Shape the Pancakes:

    Heat butter or vegetable oil in a large skillet over medium heat.
    Take a handful of the seasoned grated potatoes and shape them into pancake-sized rounds, pressing them firmly.

5. Cook:

    Place the shaped potato pancakes in the skillet, pressing them down with a spatula.
    Cook for about 5-7 minutes on each side, or until golden brown and crispy.

6. Flip:

    Carefully flip the Rösti with a spatula to cook the other side until it becomes golden brown.

7. Repeat:

    Repeat the process with the remaining grated potatoes until all the Rösti are cooked.

8. Serve:

   Once cooked, transfer the Rösti to a plate lined with paper towels to absorb any excess oil.
   Serve the Swiss Potato Pancakes warm and crispy.

9. Optional Toppings:

   Rösti can be served on its own or topped with various ingredients such as sour cream, applesauce, or smoked salmon.

Rösti is a versatile and delicious dish, perfect for breakfast or as a side dish. Enjoy the crispy exterior and tender interior of these Swiss Potato Pancakes!

Hackbraten (German Meatloaf)

Ingredients:

For the Meatloaf:

- 1.5 pounds (700g) ground beef (or a mixture of beef and pork)
- 1 onion, finely chopped
- 2 cloves garlic, minced
- 1 cup (100g) breadcrumbs
- 2/3 cup (160ml) milk
- 2 large eggs
- 2 tablespoons ketchup
- 1 tablespoon Dijon mustard
- 1 teaspoon dried thyme
- 1 teaspoon dried oregano
- Salt and pepper, to taste

For the Glaze:

- 1/4 cup (60ml) ketchup
- 1 tablespoon brown sugar
- 1 tablespoon apple cider vinegar

Instructions:

1. Preheat the Oven:

    Preheat your oven to 375°F (190°C).

2. Prepare the Meatloaf Mixture:

    In a large bowl, combine the ground beef, chopped onion, minced garlic, breadcrumbs, milk, eggs, ketchup, Dijon mustard, dried thyme, dried oregano, salt, and pepper.
    Mix the ingredients until well combined.

3. Shape the Meatloaf:

    Transfer the meatloaf mixture to a greased or lined baking dish.
    Shape it into a loaf, ensuring it's evenly distributed in the dish.

4. Make the Glaze:

In a small bowl, mix together ketchup, brown sugar, and apple cider vinegar to create the glaze.

5. Glaze the Meatloaf:

    Brush the glaze over the top of the meatloaf, ensuring an even coating.

6. Bake:

    Place the baking dish in the preheated oven.
    Bake for approximately 45-55 minutes or until the meatloaf is cooked through and has a golden-brown exterior.

7. Rest and Slice:

    Allow the Hackbraten to rest for a few minutes before slicing.

8. Serve:

    Slice the meatloaf and serve it warm.
    It goes well with mashed potatoes, vegetables, or a side salad.

Enjoy this classic German Meatloaf, Hackbraten, with its savory flavors and comforting appeal!

Hühnerfrikassee (Creamy Chicken Fricassee)

Ingredients:

- 1 whole chicken (about 3-4 pounds), cut into pieces
- 1 onion, finely chopped
- 2 carrots, sliced
- 2 celery stalks, sliced
- 1 leek, cleaned and sliced
- 1 bay leaf
- 6-8 whole peppercorns
- Salt, to taste
- 4 tablespoons butter
- 1/2 cup (60g) all-purpose flour
- 1 cup (240ml) white wine
- 2 cups (480ml) chicken broth
- 1 cup (240ml) heavy cream
- 1 teaspoon Dijon mustard
- Juice of half a lemon
- Chopped fresh parsley, for garnish

Instructions:

1. Prepare the Chicken:

   Season the chicken pieces with salt.
   In a large pot, place the chicken, chopped onion, sliced carrots, sliced celery, sliced leek, bay leaf, and whole peppercorns.
   Cover with water, bring to a boil, then reduce the heat to a simmer. Cook until the chicken is tender, about 30-40 minutes.

2. Make the Roux:

   In a separate pot, melt butter over medium heat.
   Stir in the flour to create a roux, cooking for a few minutes until it turns golden brown.

3. Add Liquid:

   Gradually add the white wine, stirring continuously to avoid lumps.
   Slowly pour in the chicken broth while stirring, allowing the mixture to thicken.

4. Creamy Sauce:

　　Pour in the heavy cream and continue to stir until the sauce is smooth and creamy.
　　Add the Dijon mustard and lemon juice. Stir to combine.

5. Finish Cooking Chicken:

　　Remove the chicken pieces from the broth and add them to the creamy sauce.
　　Discard the bay leaf and peppercorns.
　　Simmer the chicken in the creamy sauce for an additional 10-15 minutes, allowing the flavors to meld.

6. Garnish and Serve:

　　Garnish the Hühnerfrikassee with chopped fresh parsley before serving.
　　Serve the creamy chicken fricassee over rice, noodles, or with crusty bread.

Hühnerfrikassee is a comforting and elegant dish, perfect for a hearty meal. Enjoy the rich and creamy flavors of this classic German recipe!

Grünkohl mit Pinkel (Kale with Smoked Sausage)

Ingredients:

- 2 pounds (about 1 kg) fresh kale, washed and chopped

- 1 pound (about 500g) Pinkel sausage (or substitute with another smoked sausage)
- 1/2 pound (about 250g) smoked bacon, diced
- 1 large onion, finely chopped
- 2 cloves garlic, minced
- 4 medium-sized potatoes, peeled and diced
- 2 tablespoons vegetable oil or bacon fat
- 1 bay leaf
- Salt and pepper, to taste
- 1 teaspoon caraway seeds (optional)
- 1 cup (240ml) vegetable or chicken broth
- Mustard, for serving

Instructions:

1. Prepare the Kale:

   Wash the fresh kale thoroughly and remove tough stems. Chop the leaves into bite-sized pieces.

2. Cook the Kale:

   In a large pot, bring salted water to a boil.
   Add the chopped kale to the boiling water and blanch for about 5-7 minutes until tender. Drain and set aside.

3. Cook the Pinkel Sausage:

   If using raw Pinkel sausage, cook it according to the package instructions. If using pre-cooked Pinkel, you can slice it into rounds.

4. Brown Bacon and Onions:

   In a large skillet or Dutch oven, heat vegetable oil or bacon fat over medium heat.
   Add diced bacon and cook until it starts to brown.
   Add finely chopped onions and minced garlic. Sauté until the onions are translucent.

5. Add Potatoes:

Add the diced potatoes to the skillet and cook for a few minutes until they begin to brown.

6. Combine Ingredients:

    Stir in the blanched kale, bay leaf, salt, pepper, and caraway seeds (if using). Pour in the vegetable or chicken broth and bring the mixture to a simmer.

7. Simmer:

    Cover the skillet or pot, reduce the heat to low, and let the mixture simmer for about 30-40 minutes or until the potatoes are tender.

8. Add Sausage:

    Add the cooked Pinkel sausage to the kale mixture. If the sausage is pre-cooked, add it towards the end to heat through.

9. Adjust Seasoning:

    Taste and adjust the seasoning, adding more salt and pepper if needed.

10. Serve:

    Remove the bay leaf before serving.
    Serve Grünkohl mit Pinkel hot, with mustard on the side.

This hearty and warming dish is a favorite during the colder months in northern Germany. Enjoy the rich flavors of kale, smoked sausage, and bacon in this comforting and traditional recipe!

Erbsensuppe (Pea Soup)

Ingredients:

- 2 cups (400g) dried split peas

- 1 ham hock or smoked pork shank
- 1 onion, finely chopped
- 2 carrots, peeled and diced
- 2 celery stalks, diced
- 2 cloves garlic, minced
- 1 bay leaf
- 1 teaspoon dried thyme
- Salt and pepper, to taste
- 6 cups (1.5 liters) vegetable or chicken broth
- 2 tablespoons vegetable oil
- Chopped fresh parsley, for garnish (optional)
- Croutons, for serving (optional)

Instructions:

1. Rinse the Split Peas:

   Rinse the dried split peas under cold running water and drain.

2. Sauté Vegetables:

   In a large pot, heat vegetable oil over medium heat.
   Add chopped onions, diced carrots, diced celery, and minced garlic. Sauté until the vegetables are softened.

3. Add Split Peas:

   Add the rinsed split peas to the pot and stir to combine with the sautéed vegetables.

4. Add Ham Hock:

   Place the ham hock or smoked pork shank in the pot.
   Pour in the vegetable or chicken broth.

5. Season:

   Add the bay leaf, dried thyme, salt, and pepper to taste.
   Stir the ingredients and bring the soup to a boil.

6. Simmer:

   Reduce the heat to low, cover the pot, and let the soup simmer for about 1 to 1.5 hours or until the split peas are tender.

7. Remove Ham Hock:

   Once the split peas are tender, remove the ham hock or smoked pork shank from the pot.

8. Shred Ham:

   Allow the ham hock to cool slightly, then shred the meat and return it to the pot.

9. Adjust Seasoning:

   Taste the soup and adjust the seasoning if needed, adding more salt and pepper if desired.

10. Serve:

    Ladle the Erbsensuppe into bowls.
    Garnish with chopped fresh parsley and serve with croutons if desired.

Enjoy this comforting and flavorful Erbsensuppe, especially on chilly days. The combination of split peas and smoky ham creates a delicious and satisfying soup!

Lebkuchen (German Gingerbread Cookies)

Ingredients:

For the Cookies:

- 2 cups (250g) all-purpose flour
- 1/2 cup (60g) ground almonds
- 1/2 cup (120g) honey
- 1/3 cup (80g) brown sugar
- 1/4 cup (30g) candied orange peel, finely chopped
- 1/4 cup (30g) candied lemon peel, finely chopped
- 1 teaspoon ground cinnamon
- 1/2 teaspoon ground cloves
- 1/2 teaspoon ground allspice
- 1/2 teaspoon ground nutmeg
- 1/2 teaspoon baking soda
- 1/4 teaspoon salt
- 1 large egg
- 1 tablespoon (15ml) milk

For the Glaze:

- 1 cup (120g) powdered sugar
- 2 tablespoons (30ml) lemon juice
- 1 teaspoon lemon zest

Instructions:

1. Prepare the Dough:

    In a large bowl, combine the flour, ground almonds, cinnamon, cloves, allspice, nutmeg, baking soda, and salt. Set aside.
    In a saucepan, warm the honey and brown sugar over low heat until the sugar dissolves. Remove from heat and let it cool slightly.
    Add the honey mixture, chopped candied orange peel, chopped candied lemon peel, egg, and milk to the dry ingredients. Mix until well combined.
    Cover the dough and let it rest in the refrigerator for at least 1 hour or overnight.

2. Preheat the Oven:

    Preheat your oven to 350°F (175°C).
    Line baking sheets with parchment paper.

3. Shape the Cookies:

Lightly flour your hands and roll the dough into 1-inch balls.
Place the balls on the prepared baking sheets, leaving some space between each.

4. Bake:

    Bake in the preheated oven for about 10-12 minutes or until the edges are lightly browned.
    Allow the cookies to cool on the baking sheets for a few minutes before transferring them to a wire rack to cool completely.

5. Make the Glaze:

    In a small bowl, whisk together powdered sugar, lemon juice, and lemon zest until smooth.

6. Glaze the Cookies:

    Once the cookies are completely cooled, dip the tops of the cookies into the glaze or drizzle the glaze over them.
    Allow the glaze to set before serving.

7. Optional Decoration:

    You can decorate with additional candied orange or lemon peel on top of the glaze if desired.

Enjoy these homemade Lebkuchen cookies with their warm and aromatic spices, perfect for the holiday season!

Spätzle (Egg Noodles)

Ingredients:

- 2 cups (250g) all-purpose flour
- 4 large eggs
- 1/2 cup (120ml) milk
- 1/2 teaspoon salt
- Water, for boiling

Instructions:

1. Prepare the Dough:

    In a large mixing bowl, combine the flour and salt.
    Make a well in the center of the flour mixture and crack the eggs into it.
    Pour in the milk.

2. Mix the Dough:

    Gradually incorporate the flour into the wet ingredients, mixing well until you have a smooth and thick batter. The consistency should be thicker than pancake batter but not as stiff as traditional pasta dough.

3. Let the Dough Rest:

    Allow the dough to rest for about 15-20 minutes. This allows the gluten to relax and results in better-textured Spätzle.

4. Boil Water:

    Bring a large pot of salted water to a boil.

5. Form the Noodles:

    There are different methods to form Spätzle. You can use a Spätzle maker or press, a colander with large holes, or a wooden board and knife.
    - Using a Spätzle Maker/Press:
        Place the Spätzle maker or press over the boiling water.
        Pour a portion of the batter into the press and slide it back and forth, allowing small droplets of dough to fall into the boiling water.
    - Using a Colander:
        Hold the colander over the boiling water.

Pour a portion of the batter onto the colander, and use a spatula or the back of a spoon to push small pieces of dough through the holes.
- Using a Wooden Board and Knife:
Spread a portion of the batter onto a wet wooden board.
Use a knife to cut small pieces of dough and push them into the boiling water.

6. Cook the Spätzle:

The Spätzle will rise to the surface when they are cooked. Allow them to cook for an additional 1-2 minutes after they float to ensure they are done.

7. Drain and Serve:

Use a slotted spoon to remove the cooked Spätzle from the water and drain them.
Serve the Spätzle as a side dish with your favorite sauce, or incorporate them into various recipes.

Enjoy your homemade Spätzle, a delightful addition to German cuisine!

Labskaus (Corned Beef Hash)

Ingredients:

- 1 can (about 340g) corned beef, finely chopped
- 4 large potatoes, peeled and diced
- 2 onions, finely chopped
- 2 pickled beets, finely chopped
- 4 large eggs (optional)
- 4 pickles, sliced, for garnish
- Butter or oil for cooking
- Salt and pepper to taste

Instructions:

1. Boil Potatoes:

   In a large pot, boil the diced potatoes until they are tender. Drain and set aside.

2. Sauté Onions:

   In a large skillet, sauté the finely chopped onions in butter or oil until they are soft and translucent.

3. Add Corned Beef:

   Add the finely chopped corned beef to the skillet with the onions. Cook for a few minutes until the beef is heated through.

4. Mash Potatoes:

   Mash the boiled potatoes and add them to the skillet with the corned beef and onions. Mix well.

5. Add Beets:

   Stir in the finely chopped pickled beets and continue to cook, allowing the flavors to meld.

6. Season:

   Season the Labskaus with salt and pepper to taste. Adjust the seasoning according to your preference.

7. Fry Eggs (Optional):

   In a separate pan, fry eggs to your liking. Traditional Labskaus is often served with a fried egg on top.

8. Serve:

   Plate the Labskaus and top each portion with a fried egg (if using).
   Garnish with sliced pickles on the side.

Labskaus is often enjoyed with rye bread or hardtack. It has a unique combination of flavors and textures, making it a hearty and satisfying dish. The addition of a fried egg on top adds richness to the meal. Enjoy your Labskaus!

Leberknödel Suppe (Liver Dumpling Soup)

Ingredients:

For the Liver Dumplings:

- 250g (about 1/2 lb) chicken or pork liver, finely chopped
- 1 small onion, finely chopped
- 1/2 cup (50g) breadcrumbs
- 1/4 cup (60ml) milk
- 2 tablespoons butter
- 1 egg
- 2 tablespoons fresh parsley, chopped
- Salt and pepper to taste
- Nutmeg, a pinch (optional)

For the Broth:

- 1.5 liters (6 cups) beef or vegetable broth
- 1 carrot, sliced
- 1 leek, sliced
- 1 celery stalk, sliced
- Fresh parsley, chopped, for garnish
- Salt and pepper to taste

Instructions:

1. Prepare the Liver Dumplings:

> In a pan, sauté the finely chopped onions in butter until they are translucent. Allow them to cool.
> In a bowl, combine the chopped liver, sautéed onions, breadcrumbs, milk, egg, chopped parsley, salt, pepper, and nutmeg (if using). Mix well until it forms a consistent mixture.
> Shape the mixture into small dumplings, about the size of a walnut.

2. Cook the Liver Dumplings:

Bring a pot of water to a simmer. Drop the liver dumplings into the simmering water and cook for about 10 minutes until they float to the surface. Remove them with a slotted spoon and set aside.

3. Prepare the Broth:

In a separate pot, bring the beef or vegetable broth to a boil.
Add the sliced carrot, leek, and celery to the boiling broth. Simmer until the vegetables are tender.
Season the broth with salt and pepper to taste.

4. Serve:

Ladle the hot broth with vegetables into serving bowls.
Add a few liver dumplings to each bowl.
Garnish with chopped fresh parsley.

Liver Dumpling Soup is often served as a comforting and hearty starter in German cuisine. The liver dumplings add a rich and savory flavor to the broth, creating a delicious and satisfying soup. Enjoy your Leberknödel Suppe!

Schwarzwälder Kirschtorte (Black Forest Cake)

Ingredients:

For the Chocolate Sponge Cake:

- 1 cup (200g) granulated sugar
- 1 cup (130g) all-purpose flour
- 1/2 cup (60g) unsweetened cocoa powder
- 1 teaspoon baking powder
- 1/2 teaspoon baking soda
- 1/2 teaspoon salt
- 2 large eggs
- 1/2 cup (120ml) whole milk
- 1/4 cup (60ml) vegetable oil
- 2 teaspoons vanilla extract
- 1/2 cup (120ml) boiling water

For the Cherry Filling:

- 2 cups (about 500g) fresh or canned cherries, pitted
- 1/4 cup (50g) granulated sugar
- 1 tablespoon cornstarch
- 1 tablespoon lemon juice

For the Whipped Cream Frosting:

- 2 cups (480ml) heavy cream, chilled
- 1/2 cup (60g) powdered sugar
- 1 teaspoon vanilla extract
- 2 tablespoons cherry schnapps (optional)

For Garnish:

- Chocolate shavings or grated chocolate
- Maraschino cherries

Instructions:

1. Chocolate Sponge Cake:

Preheat your oven to 350°F (175°C). Grease and flour two 9-inch (23cm) round cake pans.

In a large mixing bowl, whisk together sugar, flour, cocoa powder, baking powder, baking soda, and salt.

Add eggs, milk, oil, and vanilla extract. Mix until well combined.

Stir in the boiling water. The batter will be thin.

Divide the batter evenly between the prepared pans.

Bake in the preheated oven for 30-35 minutes or until a toothpick inserted into the center comes out clean.

Allow the cakes to cool in the pans for 10 minutes, then transfer them to a wire rack to cool completely.

2. Cherry Filling:

In a saucepan, combine cherries, sugar, cornstarch, and lemon juice.

Cook over medium heat until the mixture thickens and the cherries release their juices.

Allow the cherry filling to cool completely.

3. Whipped Cream Frosting:

In a chilled mixing bowl, whip the heavy cream until soft peaks form.

Add powdered sugar, vanilla extract, and cherry schnapps (if using). Continue whipping until stiff peaks form.

4. Assemble the Black Forest Cake:

Place one chocolate cake layer on a serving plate.

Spread a layer of whipped cream frosting over the cake.

Spoon half of the cherry filling over the whipped cream.

Place the second chocolate cake layer on top.

Frost the top and sides of the cake with the remaining whipped cream.

Decorate the cake with chocolate shavings or grated chocolate.

Garnish with maraschino cherries.

5. Chill:

Refrigerate the Black Forest Cake for at least 2 hours before serving to allow the flavors to meld.

Serve this classic Schwarzwälder Kirschtorte and enjoy the delicious combination of chocolate, cherries, and whipped cream!

Gulaschsuppe (Goulash Soup)

Ingredients:

- 1.5 lbs (700g) beef stew meat, cut into bite-sized pieces
- 2 tablespoons vegetable oil
- 2 large onions, finely chopped
- 3 cloves garlic, minced
- 2 tablespoons sweet paprika
- 1 teaspoon caraway seeds
- 1 teaspoon dried marjoram
- 1 red bell pepper, diced
- 1 yellow bell pepper, diced
- 2 tablespoons tomato paste
- 1 tablespoon all-purpose flour
- 1 tablespoon red wine vinegar
- 1 can (14 oz/400g) diced tomatoes, undrained
- 6 cups (1.5 liters) beef broth
- 2 bay leaves
- Salt and black pepper to taste
- 2 large potatoes, peeled and diced
- Chopped fresh parsley for garnish
- Sour cream for serving (optional)

Instructions:

1. Brown the Meat:

    In a large pot, heat the vegetable oil over medium-high heat.
    Add the beef stew meat and brown it on all sides. Remove the meat and set it aside.

2. Sauté Onions and Garlic:

    In the same pot, add the chopped onions and sauté until they become translucent.
    Add minced garlic and sauté for another minute.

3. Add Spices:

Stir in sweet paprika, caraway seeds, and dried marjoram. Cook for a couple of minutes to release the flavors.

4. Add Bell Peppers and Tomato Paste:

    Add the diced red and yellow bell peppers to the pot.
    Stir in the tomato paste and cook for a few minutes.

5. Coat with Flour:

    Sprinkle the flour over the vegetables and stir to coat them.

6. Deglaze with Red Wine Vinegar:

    Pour in the red wine vinegar and deglaze the pot, scraping up any browned bits from the bottom.

7. Return Meat to Pot:

    Return the browned beef stew meat to the pot and mix well.

8. Add Tomatoes and Broth:

    Pour in the diced tomatoes with their juice.
    Add beef broth, bay leaves, salt, and black pepper. Stir to combine.

9. Simmer:

    Bring the soup to a boil, then reduce the heat to low, cover, and let it simmer for about 1.5 to 2 hours until the meat is tender.

10. Add Potatoes:

    Add the diced potatoes and continue simmering until the potatoes are cooked through.

11. Adjust Seasoning:

    Taste and adjust the seasoning as needed. You can add more salt, pepper, or paprika according to your preference.

12. Serve:

    Remove the bay leaves before serving.
    Ladle the Gulaschsuppe into bowls, garnish with chopped fresh parsley, and serve with a dollop of sour cream if desired.

Enjoy your hearty and comforting Goulash Soup!

Himmel und Erde (Heaven and Earth - Potatoes and Apples)

Ingredients:

- 1.5 lbs (about 700g) potatoes, peeled and diced
- 2 apples, peeled, cored, and diced
- 1 large onion, finely chopped
- 4 slices of bacon, diced
- 2 tablespoons butter
- Salt and pepper to taste
- Chopped fresh parsley for garnish (optional)

Instructions:

1. Boil Potatoes:

    In a pot, bring salted water to a boil.
    Add the diced potatoes and cook until they are fork-tender. Drain and set aside.

2. Sauté Bacon and Onions:

    In a large skillet, sauté the diced bacon until it becomes crispy.
    Add the finely chopped onions and cook until they are soft and translucent.

3. Add Apples:

    Stir in the diced apples and cook for a few minutes until they are slightly softened.

4. Combine Potatoes:

    Add the boiled and drained potatoes to the skillet. Mix well to combine all the ingredients.

5. Add Butter:

    Add the butter to the skillet and continue cooking until the butter melts and coats the potatoes, apples, bacon, and onions.

6. Season:

Season the dish with salt and pepper according to your taste. Mix well to distribute the flavors evenly.

7. Serve:

   Transfer the Himmel und Erde to a serving dish.
   Garnish with chopped fresh parsley if desired.

Himmel und Erde is a versatile dish that can be served as a side dish or a light main course. The combination of savory bacon, tender potatoes, and sweet apples creates a delicious and balanced flavor profile. Enjoy this traditional German dish!

Quarkkuchen (German Cheesecake)

Ingredients:

For the Crust:

- 1 1/2 cups (180g) all-purpose flour
- 1/2 cup (100g) granulated sugar
- 1/2 cup (115g) unsalted butter, softened
- 1 egg yolk
- 1 teaspoon vanilla extract
- A pinch of salt

For the Cheesecake Filling:

- 4 cups (about 1 kg) quark (German-style fresh cheese)
- 1 cup (200g) granulated sugar
- 4 large eggs, separated
- 1/4 cup (30g) all-purpose flour
- 1 teaspoon vanilla extract
- Zest of 1 lemon
- Juice of 1/2 lemon

Instructions:

1. Preheat the Oven:

    Preheat your oven to 350°F (180°C). Grease a 9-inch (23cm) springform pan.

2. Make the Crust:

    In a mixing bowl, combine the flour, sugar, softened butter, egg yolk, vanilla extract, and a pinch of salt.
    Mix the ingredients until a dough forms.
    Press the dough evenly into the bottom of the prepared springform pan.

3. Prepare the Cheesecake Filling:

In a large mixing bowl, combine the quark, sugar, egg yolks, flour, vanilla extract, lemon zest, and lemon juice.
Mix until well combined.

4. Beat Egg Whites:

    In a separate clean bowl, beat the egg whites until stiff peaks form.

5. Fold in Egg Whites:

    Gently fold the beaten egg whites into the quark mixture until well combined.

6. Assemble and Bake:

    Pour the quark mixture over the crust in the springform pan.
    Smooth the top with a spatula.

7. Bake:

    Bake in the preheated oven for approximately 50-60 minutes or until the cheesecake is set and the top is golden brown.

8. Cool and Serve:

    Allow the Quarkkuchen to cool in the springform pan for about 15-20 minutes. Release the sides of the springform pan and let the cheesecake cool completely before slicing.

9. Optional: Garnish:

    Garnish the cooled Quarkkuchen with fresh berries or a dusting of powdered sugar before serving, if desired.

Enjoy this delicious and creamy German Cheesecake! Quarkkuchen is known for its light and fluffy texture, making it a delightful treat for any occasion.

Dampfnudeln (Steamed Sweet Dumplings)

Ingredients:

For the Dough:

- 3 cups (375g) all-purpose flour
- 1 cup (240ml) lukewarm milk
- 2 tablespoons (30g) unsalted butter, melted
- 2 tablespoons granulated sugar
- 1 packet (2 1/4 teaspoons) active dry yeast
- 1/2 teaspoon salt

For the Caramelized Bottom:

- 1/2 cup (115g) unsalted butter
- 1/2 cup (100g) granulated sugar

For Steaming:

- 1 cup (240ml) water

Instructions:

1. Prepare the Dough:

    In a small bowl, combine lukewarm milk, sugar, and active dry yeast. Let it sit for about 5-10 minutes until it becomes frothy.
    In a large mixing bowl, combine the flour and salt. Make a well in the center.
    Pour the yeast mixture and melted butter into the well.
    Mix until a dough forms. Knead the dough on a floured surface until it becomes smooth.
    Place the dough back in the bowl, cover it with a kitchen towel, and let it rise in a warm place for about 1-2 hours or until it doubles in size.

2. Shape the Dumplings:

    Once the dough has risen, divide it into small portions and shape them into round dumplings.

3. Caramelize the Bottom:

    In a large, deep skillet or pot with a tight-fitting lid, melt the butter over medium heat.
    Sprinkle sugar evenly over the melted butter.
    Place the shaped dumplings into the skillet, arranging them in a single layer.

4. Steam the Dumplings:

    Add water to the skillet, making sure it doesn't touch the dumplings.
    Cover the skillet with the lid and steam the dumplings over medium heat for about 15-20 minutes or until they are cooked through and have a golden caramelized bottom.

5. Serve:

    Carefully remove the dumplings from the skillet and place them on a serving plate.
    Serve the Dampfnudeln warm, and you can optionally dust them with powdered sugar before serving.

Dampfnudeln are best enjoyed fresh and warm. The combination of the soft, steamed dumplings with the caramelized bottom creates a delightful texture and flavor. You can serve them with vanilla sauce, fruit compote, or enjoy them on their own.

Heringsalat (Herring Salad)

Ingredients:

- 1 jar (about 200g) pickled herring fillets, drained and chopped
- 2 apples, peeled and diced
- 1 onion, finely chopped
- 1 dill pickle, diced
- 2 boiled potatoes, diced
- 2 tablespoons mayonnaise
- 1 tablespoon sour cream
- 1 tablespoon white wine vinegar
- Salt and black pepper to taste
- Chopped fresh dill for garnish (optional)

Instructions:

1. Prepare the Herring:

    Drain the pickled herring fillets and chop them into bite-sized pieces.

2. Combine Ingredients:

    In a large bowl, combine the chopped herring, diced apples, finely chopped onion, diced dill pickle, and boiled potatoes.

3. Prepare Dressing:

    In a separate bowl, whisk together mayonnaise, sour cream, and white wine vinegar.
    Season the dressing with salt and black pepper to taste.

4. Mix and Chill:

    Pour the dressing over the herring mixture and toss everything together until well combined.

Cover the bowl and refrigerate the Heringsalat for at least 1-2 hours to allow the flavors to meld.

5. Serve:

    Before serving, give the salad a gentle toss.
    Garnish with chopped fresh dill, if desired.

6. Optional Variations:

    You can customize the salad by adding ingredients like capers, boiled eggs, or mustard for additional flavor.

7. Serving Suggestions:

    Serve Heringsalat as a refreshing side dish at picnics, barbecues, or alongside hearty German meals.

This Herring Salad combines the brininess of pickled herring with the sweetness of apples and the creaminess of the dressing, creating a flavorful and satisfying dish. Enjoy it as part of your German culinary experience!

Reibekuchen (Potato Pancakes)

Ingredients:

- 4 large potatoes, peeled and grated
- 1 onion, finely grated
- 2 eggs
- 3 tablespoons all-purpose flour
- Salt and pepper to taste
- Vegetable oil for frying
- Applesauce or sour cream for serving (optional)

Instructions:

Prepare Potatoes:
- Peel and grate the potatoes using a box grater. Place the grated potatoes in a clean kitchen towel and squeeze out excess moisture.

Combine Ingredients:
- In a mixing bowl, combine the grated potatoes, finely grated onion, eggs, flour, salt, and pepper. Mix well until all ingredients are evenly combined.

Heat Oil:
- In a large skillet, heat vegetable oil over medium-high heat.

Form Pancakes:
- Take a portion of the potato mixture in your hands, form it into a flat pancake shape, and carefully place it in the hot oil. Repeat with more portions, leaving some space between each pancake.

Fry Until Golden Brown:
- Fry the pancakes until the edges are golden brown, about 3-4 minutes on each side. Adjust the heat if necessary to prevent burning.

Drain Excess Oil:
- Once the Reibekuchen are golden brown on both sides, transfer them to a plate lined with paper towels to drain any excess oil.

Serve:
- Serve the Reibekuchen hot. They can be enjoyed on their own or with applesauce or sour cream on the side.

Optional Garnish:
- Garnish with additional salt or pepper if desired.

Reibekuchen are a delicious and comforting dish, often enjoyed during the colder months or at festive occasions. They can be served as a side dish, snack, or even as a main course. The crispy exterior and tender interior make them a favorite among many.

Kartoffelkloesse (Potato Dumplings)

Ingredients:

- 2.5 pounds (about 1.1 kg) starchy potatoes, peeled and boiled
- 1 cup (about 120g) all-purpose flour
- 2 large eggs
- 1 teaspoon salt
- 1/2 teaspoon ground nutmeg (optional)
- Butter or breadcrumbs for serving (optional)

Instructions:

Boil Potatoes:
- Peel the potatoes and boil them until they are tender. Drain and let them cool slightly.

Mash Potatoes:
- Mash the boiled potatoes while they are still warm. You can use a potato masher or a ricer for a finer texture.

Prepare the Dough:
- In a large mixing bowl, combine the mashed potatoes, flour, eggs, salt, and nutmeg (if using). Mix the ingredients until a dough forms.

Form Dumplings:
- Wet your hands to prevent sticking, and form the potato mixture into golf ball-sized dumplings.

Boil Water:
- Bring a large pot of salted water to a gentle boil.

Cook Dumplings:
- Carefully place the potato dumplings into the boiling water. Reduce the heat to a simmer and cook the dumplings for about 15-20 minutes, or until they float to the surface.

Serve:
- Use a slotted spoon to remove the dumplings from the water. Optionally, roll them in butter or breadcrumbs before serving.

Optional Serving Suggestions:
- Kartoffelklöße can be served as a side dish with various main courses, particularly those with rich gravies or sauces.

These Kartoffelklöße are soft and flavorful, making them a comforting and versatile accompaniment to a variety of dishes. Enjoy them as part of your German culinary experience!

Zwiebelkuchen (Onion Tart)

Ingredients:

For the Dough:

- 2 cups (250g) all-purpose flour
- 1 teaspoon active dry yeast
- 1/2 teaspoon salt
- 1 teaspoon sugar
- 2/3 cup (160ml) warm milk
- 2 tablespoons vegetable oil

For the Filling:

- 3 large onions, thinly sliced
- 200g bacon, diced
- 2 tablespoons vegetable oil
- 3 large eggs
- 1 cup (240ml) sour cream
- Salt and pepper to taste
- 1 teaspoon caraway seeds (optional)

Instructions:

1. Prepare the Dough:

    In a bowl, combine warm milk, sugar, and yeast. Let it sit for 5-10 minutes until frothy.
    In a large mixing bowl, combine flour and salt. Add the yeast mixture and vegetable oil. Knead the dough until smooth. Cover and let it rise in a warm place for about 1 hour.

2. Preheat Oven:

    Preheat the oven to 375°F (190°C).

3. Prepare the Filling:

In a large skillet, heat vegetable oil over medium heat. Add the sliced onions and cook until softened and lightly browned.
Add diced bacon to the skillet and cook until it's slightly crispy. Remove from heat and let it cool.

4. Roll Out the Dough:

   Roll out the risen dough on a floured surface to fit a tart pan or baking dish.
   Transfer the rolled-out dough to the pan, pressing it into the edges.

5. Assemble the Tart:

   Spread the cooked onions and bacon evenly over the dough.

6. Prepare the Custard Filling:

   In a bowl, whisk together eggs, sour cream, salt, pepper, and caraway seeds (if using).

7. Bake:

   Pour the custard filling over the onions and bacon in the tart pan.
   Bake in the preheated oven for about 30-35 minutes or until the filling is set, and the top is golden brown.

8. Serve:

   Allow the Zwiebelkuchen to cool slightly before slicing.
   Serve warm, and enjoy!

Zwiebelkuchen is often enjoyed during the fall season and is perfect for gatherings or as a cozy comfort food. The combination of savory onions and bacon with the creamy custard filling creates a delicious and satisfying dish.

Fischbrötchen (Fish Sandwich)

Ingredients:

- 4 fish fillets (herring or cod)
- 4 small crusty buns or rolls
- 1 cup (240ml) flour
- 2 eggs, beaten
- Salt and pepper to taste
- Vegetable oil for frying
- Lemon wedges for serving
- Optional toppings: lettuce, sliced tomatoes, pickles, onions, and remoulade sauce

Instructions:

1. Prepare the Fish:

    Pat the fish fillets dry with paper towels.
    Season the fillets with salt and pepper to taste.

2. Dredge in Flour:

    Dredge each fish fillet in flour, shaking off any excess.

3. Dip in Beaten Eggs:

    Dip the floured fish fillets into the beaten eggs, ensuring they are well-coated.

4. Fry the Fish:

    In a large skillet, heat vegetable oil over medium-high heat.
    Fry the fish fillets for 2-3 minutes on each side or until they are golden brown and cooked through.
    Place the fried fillets on a plate lined with paper towels to absorb any excess oil.

5. Assemble the Sandwich:

    Cut the buns or rolls in half.
    Place a fried fish fillet on the bottom half of each bun.

6. Add Toppings:

    Add your preferred toppings such as lettuce, sliced tomatoes, pickles, and onions.

7. Serve:

    Optionally, spread remoulade sauce on the top half of the bun.
    Serve the Fischbrötchen with lemon wedges on the side.

Fischbrötchen can be customized with various toppings, and the choice of fish may vary based on personal preference and regional availability. Enjoy these delicious fish sandwiches as a quick and tasty snack, especially during a visit to the coastal areas of Germany!

Zimtsterne (Cinnamon Stars Cookies)

Ingredients:

For the Dough:

- 3 cups (300g) ground almonds
- 1 1/4 cups (150g) powdered sugar
- 1 tablespoon ground cinnamon
- 2 large egg whites
- 1 teaspoon lemon juice

For the Glaze:

- 1 cup (120g) powdered sugar
- 1-2 tablespoons lemon juice

Instructions:

Preheat your oven to 300°F (150°C). Line a baking sheet with parchment paper. In a large bowl, combine the ground almonds, powdered sugar, and ground cinnamon.

In a separate bowl, beat the egg whites until stiff peaks form. Add the lemon juice and continue to beat until glossy.

Gently fold the beaten egg whites into the almond mixture until well combined. The dough should be sticky but manageable.

Dust your work surface with powdered sugar to prevent sticking, and roll out the dough to a thickness of about 1/2 inch (1.3 cm).

Use a star-shaped cookie cutter to cut out the cookies and place them on the prepared baking sheet.

In a small bowl, mix together the powdered sugar and lemon juice to create a glaze. Brush the glaze over the tops of the cookies.

Bake in the preheated oven for about 12-15 minutes or until the edges are lightly golden.

Allow the Zimtsterne to cool on the baking sheet for a few minutes before transferring them to a wire rack to cool completely.

These cinnamon stars are not only visually appealing but also have a wonderful chewy texture and a rich, nutty flavor. Enjoy these delightful cookies as a festive treat during the holiday season!

Schupfnudeln (Potato Noodles)

Ingredients:

- 2 pounds (about 1 kg) potatoes, preferably starchy varieties
- 1 1/2 cups (about 180g) all-purpose flour
- 1 large egg
- Salt, to taste
- Nutmeg, to taste (optional)
- Butter or oil, for frying

Instructions:

Peel and boil the potatoes until they are tender. Drain and let them cool slightly. Once the potatoes are cool enough to handle, mash them or use a potato ricer to create a smooth texture.

In a large mixing bowl, combine the mashed potatoes with the flour, egg, salt, and nutmeg (if using). Mix until the ingredients come together to form a dough. The dough should be soft but not too sticky.

On a floured surface, roll portions of the dough into long, thin ropes, about 1/2 to 1 inch (1.3 to 2.5 cm) in diameter.

Cut the ropes into shorter pieces, around 2 inches (5 cm) long, and shape each piece into an elongated, tapered oval. You can also use a fork to create ridges along the length of the noodle.

Heat butter or oil in a large skillet over medium heat. Once hot, add the Schupfnudeln and cook until they are golden brown on all sides. You may need to do this in batches.

Serve the Schupfnudeln warm as a side dish, traditionally with sauerkraut, cabbage, or a hearty stew. They can also be served with sweet toppings, such as cinnamon sugar or fruit compote, for a dessert version.

Schupfnudeln are versatile and can be adapted to various dishes and flavors. They are a comforting and delicious addition to your German cuisine repertoire.

Weißwurst mit Brezn (White Sausage with Pretzel)

Weißwurst Ingredients:

- 8 Weißwurst sausages
- 1 liter water
- 1 onion, finely chopped
- 1 tablespoon salt
- 1 teaspoon white pepper
- 1/2 teaspoon mace (optional)
- Fresh parsley, chopped (for garnish)

Brezn Ingredients:

- 4 large soft pretzels
- Mustard for serving

Instructions:

Weißwurst:

In a large pot, bring water to a simmer.
Add chopped onions, salt, white pepper, and mace (if using) to the simmering water.
Carefully add the Weißwurst sausages to the pot and let them simmer for about 10 minutes. Make sure not to boil them as it can cause the skin to burst.
Remove the sausages from the water using a slotted spoon and place them on a serving plate.

Brezn:

Preheat your oven according to the pretzel package instructions.
Warm the pretzels in the oven until they are heated through.
Place the warm pretzels on the serving plate alongside the Weißwurst.

Serving:

Sprinkle chopped fresh parsley over the Weißwurst for a burst of color and flavor.
Serve the Weißwurst with warm pretzels and a side of mustard.

Traditionally, Weißwurst mit Brezn is enjoyed for breakfast or brunch. It's important to peel the skin off the Weißwurst before eating. Accompany it with a refreshing beer or a pretzel's best companion, sweet mustard.

Enjoy your Weißwurst mit Brezn!

Gemüsesuppe (Vegetable Soup)

Ingredients:

- 2 tablespoons olive oil
- 1 onion, finely chopped
- 2 cloves garlic, minced
- 2 carrots, peeled and diced
- 2 celery stalks, diced
- 1 leek, sliced (white and light green parts only)
- 1 potato, peeled and diced
- 1 zucchini, diced
- 1 cup green beans, chopped
- 1 can (14 oz) diced tomatoes (with juice)
- 8 cups vegetable broth
- 1 teaspoon dried thyme
- 1 teaspoon dried oregano
- Salt and pepper to taste
- 1 cup pasta or rice (optional)
- Fresh parsley, chopped (for garnish)

Instructions:

In a large pot, heat the olive oil over medium heat. Add the chopped onion and garlic, and sauté until they become translucent.
Add the diced carrots, celery, leek, potato, zucchini, and green beans to the pot. Stir and cook for about 5 minutes until the vegetables start to soften.
Pour in the diced tomatoes with their juice and add the vegetable broth to the pot. Bring the mixture to a boil.
Once boiling, reduce the heat to simmer and add the dried thyme, dried oregano, salt, and pepper. If you're using pasta or rice, add it at this point.
Allow the soup to simmer for about 15-20 minutes or until the vegetables are tender. If you added pasta or rice, cook until they are done.
Taste the soup and adjust the seasoning if necessary.
Ladle the vegetable soup into bowls, and garnish with fresh chopped parsley.
Serve hot and enjoy your comforting Gemüsesuppe!

Feel free to customize the recipe by adding your favorite vegetables or herbs. It's a great way to make a healthy and flavorful meal, especially during colder months.

Maultaschen (Swabian Dumplings)

Ingredients:

For the Dough:

- 3 cups all-purpose flour
- 4 large eggs
- 1/2 teaspoon salt
- Water (as needed to form a smooth dough)

For the Filling:

- 1/2 pound ground beef or pork
- 1/2 pound cooked and chopped spinach (can use frozen, drained spinach)
- 1 onion, finely chopped
- 2 cloves garlic, minced
- Salt and pepper to taste
- Nutmeg, a pinch (optional)
- Fresh parsley, chopped

Other Ingredients:

- Beef or vegetable broth for cooking

Instructions:

Dough Preparation:

In a large bowl, combine the flour, eggs, and salt.
Mix the ingredients, adding water gradually until you form a smooth, elastic dough.
Cover the dough and let it rest for about 30 minutes.

Filling Preparation:

In a pan, cook the ground meat until browned. Drain excess fat if needed.
Add chopped onions and garlic to the pan and sauté until softened.
Stir in the cooked and chopped spinach.
Season the mixture with salt, pepper, nutmeg (if using), and fresh chopped parsley.
Let the filling cool down.

Assembling Maultaschen:

> Roll out the rested dough on a floured surface until it's about 1/8 inch thick.
> Cut the rolled-out dough into squares (typically around 4x4 inches).
> Place a spoonful of the filling in the center of each square.
> Fold the squares to form triangles, sealing the edges to encase the filling.

Cooking:

> Bring a pot of salted water or broth to a simmer.
> Carefully add the Maultaschen to the simmering water and cook for about 15-20 minutes.
> Remove them from the water using a slotted spoon.

Maultaschen can be served in various ways, such as in a broth, pan-fried with butter and onions, or just on their own. They are a delicious and hearty dish with a rich cultural history in the Swabian region.

Birnen, Bohnen und Speck (Pears, Beans, and Bacon)

Ingredients:

- 500g green beans, cleaned and trimmed
- 4 ripe pears, peeled, cored, and cut into wedges
- 200g bacon, diced
- 1 onion, finely chopped
- 2 tablespoons butter
- Salt and pepper to taste
- Chopped fresh parsley for garnish

Instructions:

Prepare the Green Beans:
- Blanch the green beans in salted boiling water for about 5 minutes until they are slightly tender but still have a crunch.
- Drain the beans and set them aside.

Cook the Bacon and Onions:
- In a large pan, cook the diced bacon over medium heat until it becomes crispy.
- Add the finely chopped onion to the bacon and cook until the onion is translucent.

Add Pears and Butter:
- Add the pear wedges to the pan with the bacon and onions.
- Add the butter to the pan and stir gently to coat the pears.

Combine with Green Beans:
- Add the blanched green beans to the pan and toss everything together.
- Season with salt and pepper according to your taste.

Finish and Serve:
- Cook the mixture for a few more minutes until everything is heated through and well combined.
- Garnish with chopped fresh parsley.

"Birnen, Bohnen und Speck" can be served as a side dish alongside various main courses. The combination of sweet pears, crisp green beans, and savory bacon creates a delightful balance of flavors. It's a comforting and classic dish that showcases the simplicity and deliciousness of traditional German cuisine.

Krustenbraten (Roast Pork with Crispy Skin)

Ingredients:

- 1.5 kg (approximately 3.3 pounds) pork roast, preferably with skin on
- Salt and pepper to taste
- Caraway seeds (optional)
- Mustard for coating (preferably Dijon or whole grain)
- 2 onions, sliced
- 2 carrots, chopped
- 2 celery stalks, chopped
- 2 cloves garlic, minced
- 1 bay leaf
- 500 ml (2 cups) beef or vegetable broth
- 250 ml (1 cup) dry white wine
- 2 tablespoons vegetable oil

Instructions:

Prepare the Pork:
- Preheat the oven to 220°C (425°F).
- Score the skin of the pork roast with a sharp knife, making parallel cuts about 1 cm apart.
- Rub the pork roast with salt, pepper, and caraway seeds if desired.
- Coat the skin side with a generous layer of mustard.

Sear the Pork:
- In a large oven-safe pan or Dutch oven, heat vegetable oil over medium-high heat.
- Sear the pork roast on all sides until it develops a golden-brown color.

Prepare the Vegetables and Braising Liquid:
- Remove the seared pork from the pan and set it aside.
- In the same pan, add onions, carrots, celery, and garlic. Cook until softened.
- Pour in the white wine to deglaze the pan, scraping up any browned bits from the bottom.
- Add beef or vegetable broth and bay leaf.

Roast the Pork:
- Place the seared pork roast on top of the vegetables in the pan.
- Transfer the pan to the preheated oven and roast for about 30 minutes.

Reduce Heat for Crispy Skin:
- After 30 minutes, reduce the oven temperature to 180°C (350°F).
- Continue roasting for another 1 to 1.5 hours or until the internal temperature of the pork reaches at least 70°C (160°F).

Let it Rest:
- Once done, remove the pork from the oven and let it rest for a few minutes before slicing.

Serve:
- Slice the Krustenbraten and serve it with the roasted vegetables and pan juices.

Krustenbraten is often served with traditional side dishes like potato dumplings, sauerkraut, or red cabbage. The combination of tender pork and crispy crackling makes it a beloved dish in German cuisine.

Rhabarberkuchen (Rhubarb Cake)

Ingredients:

For the Cake:

- 250g (2 cups) all-purpose flour
- 2 teaspoons baking powder
- 1/4 teaspoon salt
- 150g (3/4 cup) unsalted butter, softened
- 200g (1 cup) granulated sugar
- 3 large eggs
- 1 teaspoon vanilla extract
- 120ml (1/2 cup) milk

For the Rhubarb Topping:

- 400g (about 3 cups) rhubarb, washed and cut into 1-inch pieces
- 60g (1/4 cup) granulated sugar

Optional Streusel Topping:

- 60g (1/4 cup) unsalted butter, melted
- 80g (1/2 cup) all-purpose flour
- 60g (1/4 cup) granulated sugar

Instructions:

Preheat the Oven:
- Preheat your oven to 180°C (350°F). Grease and flour a baking pan.

Prepare the Cake Batter:
- In a bowl, whisk together the flour, baking powder, and salt.
- In another large bowl, cream together the softened butter and sugar until light and fluffy.
- Add the eggs one at a time, beating well after each addition. Stir in the vanilla extract.
- Gradually add the dry ingredients to the wet ingredients, alternating with the milk. Mix until just combined.

Make the Rhubarb Topping:
- Toss the rhubarb pieces with sugar and set aside.

Assemble the Cake:
- Spread the cake batter evenly into the prepared baking pan.

- Arrange the rhubarb pieces on top of the batter.

Optional Streusel Topping:
- If you want to add streusel, combine the melted butter, flour, and sugar in a bowl. Sprinkle the streusel over the rhubarb.

Bake:
- Bake in the preheated oven for about 45-55 minutes or until a toothpick inserted into the center comes out clean.

Cool and Serve:
- Allow the Rhubarb Cake to cool in the pan for about 15 minutes before transferring it to a wire rack to cool completely.

Serve:
- Slice and serve the Rhubarb Cake. It can be enjoyed on its own or with a dollop of whipped cream or a scoop of vanilla ice cream.

This Rhubarb Cake is a delicious way to celebrate the vibrant flavor of rhubarb, and it's a perfect dessert for spring and early summer.

Bienenstich (Bee Sting Cake)

Ingredients:

For the Dough:

- 500g (4 cups) all-purpose flour
- 7g (2 1/4 teaspoons) active dry yeast
- 250ml (1 cup) warm milk
- 75g (1/3 cup) unsalted butter, softened
- 75g (1/3 cup) granulated sugar
- 1/2 teaspoon salt
- 2 large eggs

For the Filling:

- 500ml (2 cups) milk
- 120g (2/3 cup) granulated sugar
- 1 package (about 37g) vanilla pudding mix (for cooking)
- 3-4 tablespoons cornstarch

For the Topping:

- 150g (1 1/2 cups) sliced almonds
- 100g (1/2 cup) unsalted butter
- 100g (1/2 cup) granulated sugar
- 2 tablespoons honey
- 2 tablespoons heavy cream

Instructions:

For the Dough:

> In a small bowl, dissolve the yeast in warm milk with a pinch of sugar. Let it sit for about 5-10 minutes until it becomes frothy.
> In a large bowl, combine the flour, sugar, and salt.
> Add the yeast mixture, softened butter, and eggs to the flour mixture. Mix until a soft dough forms.
> Knead the dough on a floured surface for about 5-7 minutes until it becomes smooth.
> Place the dough in a greased bowl, cover it with a clean kitchen towel, and let it rise in a warm place for 1-2 hours or until it has doubled in size.

For the Filling:

In a saucepan, heat the milk until it's warm but not boiling.
In a separate bowl, whisk together sugar, vanilla pudding mix, and cornstarch.
Gradually whisk the dry ingredients into the warm milk, stirring constantly.
Cook the mixture over medium heat until it thickens, stirring continuously.
Remove from heat and let it cool.

For the Topping:

In a saucepan, melt butter, sugar, honey, and heavy cream over medium heat.
Stir in the sliced almonds and cook until the mixture caramelizes slightly.
Remove from heat and let it cool.

Assemble the Cake:

Preheat the oven to 180°C (350°F).
Roll out the risen dough and place it in a greased baking pan.
Spread the cooled vanilla pudding filling over the dough.
Pour the caramelized almond topping over the filling.

Bake:

Bake in the preheated oven for about 25-30 minutes or until the edges are golden brown.
Let the Bienenstich cool before slicing and serving.

Bienenstich is a delightful treat with a combination of textures and flavors, making it a favorite among those who enjoy German pastries.

Schmandkuchen (Sour Cream Cake)

Ingredients:

For the Cake:

- 200g (1 cup) unsalted butter, softened
- 200g (1 cup) granulated sugar
- 4 large eggs
- 1 teaspoon vanilla extract
- 250g (2 cups) all-purpose flour
- 2 teaspoons baking powder
- 250g (1 cup) sour cream

For the Topping:

- 250g (1 cup) sour cream
- 50g (1/4 cup) granulated sugar
- 1 teaspoon vanilla extract

Instructions:

For the Cake:

Preheat the oven to 180°C (350°F). Grease and flour a cake pan.
In a large bowl, cream together the softened butter and sugar until light and fluffy.
Add the eggs one at a time, beating well after each addition. Stir in the vanilla extract.
In a separate bowl, whisk together the flour and baking powder.
Gradually add the dry ingredients to the butter mixture, alternating with the sour cream. Begin and end with the dry ingredients. Mix until just combined.
Pour the batter into the prepared cake pan, spreading it evenly.

For the Topping:

In a bowl, mix together the sour cream, sugar, and vanilla extract.
Spoon the sour cream mixture over the cake batter, spreading it evenly.

Bake:

Bake in the preheated oven for about 30-35 minutes or until a toothpick inserted into the center comes out clean.
Allow the cake to cool in the pan for about 10 minutes before transferring it to a wire rack to cool completely.

Serve:

    Once cooled, slice and serve the Schmandkuchen.

This Sour Cream Cake is characterized by its dense yet moist texture and the tangy flavor from the sour cream. It's a delightful dessert that can be enjoyed on its own or with a dusting of powdered sugar.

Blumenkohl in Senfsauce (Cauliflower in Mustard Sauce)

Ingredients:

- 1 large cauliflower, cleaned and cut into florets
- Salt, for boiling cauliflower
- 2 tablespoons butter
- 2 tablespoons all-purpose flour
- 1 cup milk
- 2 tablespoons Dijon mustard
- 1 tablespoon whole grain mustard
- Salt and pepper, to taste
- Fresh parsley, chopped, for garnish

Instructions:

Prepare the Cauliflower:
- Bring a large pot of salted water to a boil.
- Add cauliflower florets to the boiling water and cook for about 5-7 minutes or until they are just tender. Drain and set aside.

Make the Mustard Sauce:
- In a saucepan, melt butter over medium heat.
- Add flour and whisk continuously to create a roux. Cook for 1-2 minutes to remove the raw flour taste.
- Gradually add milk, whisking constantly to avoid lumps.
- Stir in Dijon mustard and whole grain mustard.
- Continue cooking and stirring until the sauce thickens. Season with salt and pepper to taste.

Combine Cauliflower and Sauce:
- Add the cooked cauliflower to the mustard sauce, gently tossing to coat each floret with the sauce.

Serve:
- Transfer the cauliflower in mustard sauce to a serving dish.
- Garnish with chopped fresh parsley.

Enjoy:
- Serve the Blumenkohl in Senfsauce as a side dish or even as a light main course.

This dish is a wonderful way to enjoy cauliflower with a zesty mustard kick. The creamy sauce complements the mild flavor of the cauliflower, creating a delightful combination. It can be served alongside potatoes, rice, or crusty bread.

Weihnachtsplätzchen (Christmas Cookies)

Ingredients:

For the Cookies:

- 225g (1 cup) unsalted butter, softened
- 200g (1 cup) granulated sugar
- 2 large eggs
- 1 teaspoon vanilla extract
- 4 cups all-purpose flour
- 1/2 teaspoon baking powder
- 1/4 teaspoon salt

For the Icing (Optional):

- 2 cups powdered sugar
- 1-2 tablespoons milk
- Food coloring (optional)

Instructions:

For the Cookies:

Preheat the Oven:
- Preheat your oven to 180°C (350°F). Line baking sheets with parchment paper.

Cream Butter and Sugar:
- In a large bowl, cream together the softened butter and granulated sugar until light and fluffy.

Add Eggs and Vanilla:
- Add the eggs one at a time, beating well after each addition. Stir in the vanilla extract.

Combine Dry Ingredients:
- In a separate bowl, whisk together the flour, baking powder, and salt.

Mix the Dough:
- Gradually add the dry ingredients to the butter mixture, mixing until just combined. Do not overmix.

Chill the Dough:
- Divide the dough into two portions, shape them into discs, and wrap in plastic wrap. Chill the dough in the refrigerator for at least 1-2 hours.

Roll and Cut:
- Roll out the chilled dough on a floured surface to your desired thickness.

- Use festive cookie cutters to cut out shapes and place them on the prepared baking sheets.

Bake:
- Bake in the preheated oven for 8-10 minutes or until the edges are lightly golden.

Cool:
- Allow the cookies to cool on the baking sheets for a few minutes before transferring them to wire racks to cool completely.

For the Icing (Optional):

Prepare the Icing:
- In a bowl, whisk together the powdered sugar and milk until smooth. Add more milk if needed to achieve your desired consistency.

Color the Icing (Optional):
- If using food coloring, divide the icing into smaller bowls and add colors of your choice.

Decorate the Cookies:
- Once the cookies are completely cooled, use a small spatula or piping bag to decorate them with icing, and add festive sprinkles or decorations.

Let the Icing Set:
- Allow the icing to set before storing or packaging the cookies.

These Christmas cookies can be made in various shapes and decorated in endless ways. It's a fun and festive activity to share with family and friends during the holiday season.

Rinderrouladen (Beef Rolls with Bacon and Pickles)

Ingredients:

For the Rouladen:

- 4 slices of beef (about 150-200g each), thinly sliced
- Salt and pepper, to taste
- Dijon mustard
- 4 slices of bacon
- 1 large onion, finely chopped
- 4 pickles (dill or gherkin), sliced into strips
- Vegetable oil, for browning

For the Braising Liquid:

- 500ml beef broth
- 250ml red wine (optional)
- 1 onion, sliced
- 2 carrots, sliced
- 2 cloves garlic, minced
- 2 bay leaves
- 2 tablespoons tomato paste
- Salt and pepper, to taste

For Thickening (Optional):

- 2 tablespoons all-purpose flour
- 2 tablespoons butter

Instructions:

Prepare the Beef Slices:
- Pound the beef slices to make them thinner and more even.
- Season each slice with salt and pepper.
- Spread a thin layer of Dijon mustard on one side of each beef slice.

Create the Filling:
- Place a slice of bacon on each beef slice.
- Sprinkle chopped onions over the bacon.
- Lay a strip of pickle along one edge of each beef slice.

Roll the Rouladen:

- Roll up the beef slices, enclosing the filling tightly. Secure with toothpicks or kitchen twine.

Brown the Rouladen:
- Heat vegetable oil in a large, oven-safe pot or Dutch oven over medium-high heat.
- Brown the Rouladen on all sides until they develop a nice sear. Remove them from the pot and set aside.

Prepare the Braising Liquid:
- In the same pot, add sliced onions, carrots, and minced garlic. Sauté until softened.
- Add beef broth, red wine (if using), bay leaves, tomato paste, salt, and pepper. Bring to a simmer.

Braise the Rouladen:
- Return the browned Rouladen to the pot, making sure they are submerged in the liquid.
- Cover the pot and place it in a preheated oven at 180°C (350°F). Braise for about 1.5 to 2 hours or until the meat is tender.

Optional Thickening:
- If you want a thicker sauce, mix flour and butter together to form a paste. Stir this into the braising liquid and cook on the stovetop until it thickens.

Serve:
- Remove the toothpicks or twine from the Rouladen.
- Serve the Rinderrouladen with the braising liquid as a sauce.

This traditional German dish is often served with sides like red cabbage, mashed potatoes, or spaetzle. Enjoy your Rinderrouladen!

Senfeier (Mustard Eggs)

Ingredients:

- 4-6 hard-boiled eggs, peeled and halved
- 2 tablespoons butter
- 2 tablespoons all-purpose flour
- 2 cups milk
- 2 tablespoons Dijon mustard
- Salt and pepper to taste
- Chopped fresh parsley for garnish (optional)

Instructions:

Prepare Hard-Boiled Eggs:
- Hard-boil the eggs, peel them, and cut them in half lengthwise.

Make the Mustard Sauce:
- In a saucepan, melt butter over medium heat.
- Add flour and whisk continuously to create a roux. Cook for 1-2 minutes to remove the raw flour taste.
- Gradually add milk, whisking constantly to avoid lumps.
- Stir in Dijon mustard and continue cooking and stirring until the sauce thickens. Season with salt and pepper to taste.

Add Hard-Boiled Eggs:
- Gently place the halved hard-boiled eggs into the mustard sauce, ensuring they are coated with the sauce.

Warm the Eggs:
- Allow the eggs to warm in the sauce for a few minutes. Be careful not to overcook, as the eggs are already hard-boiled.

Serve:
- Spoon the eggs and mustard sauce onto plates or a serving dish.

Garnish (Optional):
- Sprinkle chopped fresh parsley on top for a burst of color and flavor.

Serve with Sides:
- Senfeier is often served with boiled potatoes or rice on the side to soak up the delicious mustard sauce.

Senfeier is a quick and tasty dish that showcases the combination of creamy mustard sauce and the richness of hard-boiled eggs. It's a popular comfort food in Germany and can be enjoyed as a main dish or a hearty side.

Wurstsalat (Sausage Salad)

Ingredients:

For the Salad:

- 300g (about 10 oz) German-style sausages (such as Fleischwurst or Lyoner), thinly sliced
- 1 red onion, thinly sliced
- 1 small cucumber, thinly sliced
- 1-2 dill pickles, thinly sliced
- 100g (about 1 cup) Emmental cheese, thinly sliced or shredded

For the Dressing:

- 3 tablespoons white wine vinegar
- 2 tablespoons vegetable oil
- 1 tablespoon mustard (Dijon or German-style)
- 1 teaspoon sugar
- Salt and pepper to taste
- Chopped fresh parsley for garnish (optional)

Instructions:

Prepare the Salad Ingredients:
- Thinly slice the sausages, red onion, cucumber, dill pickles, and Emmental cheese. You can adjust the quantities based on your preference.

Assemble the Salad:
- In a large bowl, combine the sliced sausages, red onion, cucumber, pickles, and Emmental cheese.

Make the Dressing:
- In a small bowl, whisk together white wine vinegar, vegetable oil, mustard, sugar, salt, and pepper until well combined.

Dress the Salad:
- Pour the dressing over the salad ingredients and toss everything together until well coated.

Let it Marinate:
- Allow the Wurstsalat to marinate for about 15-30 minutes in the refrigerator. This allows the flavors to meld.

Garnish (Optional):

- If desired, garnish the Wurstsalat with chopped fresh parsley before serving.

Serve:
- Serve the Wurstsalat chilled as an appetizer, light meal, or as part of a traditional German snack platter.

Wurstsalat is often enjoyed with a slice of crusty bread or as a side dish with a pretzel. It's a refreshing and flavorful dish that showcases the delicious combination of sausages and tangy dressing.

Linsensuppe (Lentil Soup)

Ingredients:

- 1 cup dry green or brown lentils, rinsed and drained
- 1 large onion, finely chopped
- 2 carrots, peeled and diced
- 2 celery stalks, diced
- 2 cloves garlic, minced
- 1 bay leaf
- 1 teaspoon dried thyme
- 1 teaspoon ground cumin
- 1 can (400g/14oz) diced tomatoes
- 6 cups vegetable or chicken broth
- Salt and pepper to taste
- 2 tablespoons olive oil
- Fresh parsley for garnish (optional)
- Lemon wedges for serving (optional)

Instructions:

Prepare the Lentils:
- Rinse the lentils under cold water and drain them.

Sauté Vegetables:
- In a large soup pot, heat olive oil over medium heat. Add chopped onion, carrots, and celery. Sauté until the vegetables are softened.

Add Garlic and Spices:
- Add minced garlic, bay leaf, thyme, and ground cumin. Sauté for another minute until fragrant.

Add Lentils and Broth:
- Add the rinsed lentils to the pot and stir to combine with the vegetables and spices.
- Pour in the diced tomatoes and vegetable or chicken broth.

Simmer:
- Bring the soup to a boil, then reduce the heat to low and let it simmer, covered, for about 30-40 minutes or until the lentils are tender.

Season:
- Season the soup with salt and pepper to taste. Adjust the seasoning as needed.

Garnish and Serve:

- Remove the bay leaf from the soup.
- Ladle the hot Lentil Soup into bowls.
- Garnish with fresh parsley and serve with lemon wedges on the side if desired.

Lentil Soup is a versatile dish, and you can customize it by adding other vegetables, such as spinach or kale. It's a wholesome and comforting soup that is not only delicious but also rich in protein and fiber. Enjoy it on its own or with a slice of crusty bread.

Stollen (German Christmas Fruitcake)

Ingredients:

For the Dough:

- 4 cups all-purpose flour
- 1/2 cup granulated sugar
- 1 package (7g) active dry yeast
- 1 cup warm milk
- 1/2 cup unsalted butter, softened
- 1/2 teaspoon salt
- 1/2 teaspoon vanilla extract
- 1/2 teaspoon almond extract
- Zest of one lemon
- Zest of one orange

For the Filling:

- 1 cup mixed candied fruits (citrus peel, cherries, etc.), chopped
- 1 cup raisins or currants
- 1 cup chopped nuts (almonds, hazelnuts, or a mix)
- 200g marzipan, optional, cut into small pieces

For Finishing:

- Powdered sugar, for dusting
- Butter, for brushing

Instructions:

Activate the Yeast:
- In a small bowl, combine warm milk and a pinch of sugar. Sprinkle the yeast over the milk and let it sit for about 5-10 minutes until it becomes frothy.

Prepare the Dough:
- In a large bowl, mix together flour, sugar, and salt. Create a well in the center.
- Pour the activated yeast mixture into the well.
- Add softened butter, vanilla extract, almond extract, lemon zest, and orange zest to the bowl.
- Mix everything together to form a dough.

Knead the Dough:
- Turn the dough out onto a floured surface and knead for about 8-10 minutes until it becomes smooth and elastic.

Add the Filling:
- Flatten the dough and spread the candied fruits, raisins or currants, nuts, and marzipan pieces evenly over the surface.
- Fold the dough over the filling and knead until the fruits and nuts are distributed throughout.

Let it Rise:
- Place the dough in a greased bowl, cover it with a kitchen towel, and let it rise in a warm place for about 1-2 hours or until it doubles in size.

Shape the Stollen:
- Punch down the risen dough and shape it into an oval or oblong loaf.
- Place the shaped Stollen on a parchment-lined baking sheet.

Final Rise:
- Cover the shaped Stollen with a kitchen towel and let it rise for an additional 30-45 minutes.

Bake:
- Preheat your oven to 350°F (180°C).
- Bake the Stollen for 30-40 minutes or until it's golden brown.

Finish:
- While the Stollen is still warm, brush it with melted butter and dust it generously with powdered sugar.

Cool and Serve:
- Allow the Stollen to cool completely before slicing and serving.

Stollen is often enjoyed during the Christmas season and can be wrapped in foil and stored for several weeks. The flavors tend to develop and improve with time. It's a festive and delightful treat that captures the spirit of German Christmas traditions.

Kaiserschmarrn (Shredded Pancakes)

Ingredients:

- 2 cups all-purpose flour
- 2 tablespoons sugar
- 1/2 teaspoon salt
- 4 large eggs, separated
- 1 1/2 cups milk
- 1 teaspoon vanilla extract
- 3 tablespoons unsalted butter
- Powdered sugar, for dusting
- Raisins (optional)
- Fruit compote or applesauce, for serving

Instructions:

Prepare the Batter:
- In a bowl, whisk together flour, sugar, and salt.
- In another bowl, whisk together egg yolks, milk, and vanilla extract.
- Gradually add the wet ingredients to the dry ingredients, whisking until you have a smooth batter.

Whip Egg Whites:
- In a separate clean, dry bowl, whip the egg whites until stiff peaks form.

Fold in Egg Whites:
- Gently fold the whipped egg whites into the pancake batter until well combined. Be careful not to deflate the egg whites.

Cook the Pancake:
- In a large, oven-proof skillet, melt butter over medium heat.
- Pour the pancake batter into the skillet and cook for a few minutes until the edges set.

Shred the Pancake:
- Using a spatula, start tearing the pancake into large pieces. You can use a fork to help shred it into smaller, bite-sized pieces.

Add Optional Raisins:
- If desired, sprinkle raisins over the shredded pancake.

Finish Cooking:
- Continue cooking and flipping the shredded pancake pieces until they are golden brown and cooked through.

Serve:

- Dust the Kaiserschmarrn with powdered sugar.
- Serve it warm with fruit compote or applesauce on the side.

Kaiserschmarrn is often served in the pan it's cooked in, and it's meant to be torn apart and enjoyed with a fork. It's a deliciously fluffy and slightly caramelized pancake that is sure to be a hit, whether served for breakfast or as a dessert.

www.ingramcontent.com/pod-product-compliance
Lightning Source LLC
LaVergne TN
LVHW081602060526
838201LV00054B/2032